Sentiments to Soothe Your Soul

Sentiments to Soothe Your Soul

Author: Carolyn Y. Hall

For additional information contact:
Carolyn Y. Hall
P.O. Box 134, Dallas, GA 30132
Email: hallpublishinggroup@yahoo.com
Website: www.hallpublishinggroup.com

Cover Designed by: Dub-G Spencer
Editors: Carolyn Hall

ISBN: 978-0-9857948-2-8

Printed in the United States of America

Dedication:

This book is dedicated to all the important people in my life that's always supported me and had my back. Please know, trust and believe that I love and appreciate each and every one of you in your own special way.

Time Piece

If I could turn back the hands of time—my initial thoughts would be to change
all the areas in my life where I went wrong, and to avoid all the costly mistakes
I've made along the way.

However, if I think about it a little longer I must admit some of the mistakes
I've made along the way have helped me to become the strong, vigilant,
determined person that I am today.

So instead of focusing on the times I've got it all WRONG—I'm going to
instead focus on the times I've got it RIGHT. And those thoughts are going to
continue to hold and comfort me whenever I find myself traveling down the
Get It All Wrong Highway again.

Because as long as I continue to live and make choices that's one destination
I'm sure I'll visit again.

Breath

As long as you have breath in your body there's opportunity to change the things and people in your life that are not contributing to your overall happiness and peace of mind.

However, remember that change is always met with resistance and dismay. Therefore, keep in mind the things in life that doesn't kill you will build you up, and make you a better, stronger, happier person.

Never stop challenging your tomorrows to be better than your yesterdays—because behind every challenge is a new opportunity for greatness.

True Love

True love doesn't hurt. It should be the calm after the storm, the peace after the commotion, and the rainbow after the rain.

When your relationship begins to feel and look like those old shoes in your closet, you know the ones that have holes in them—but they still fit well, and feel real good, that's when you know it's time to throw them away.

True Love is about giving more than you take—having more good days than bad days—and having more joy than pain.

However, when the taking outweighs the giving, and the bad days outweigh the good days, and most importantly, when the pain outweighs the joy.

It's no longer *True Love.* It's a crutch! And it's time to get up, push forward, and get your happiness back.

Never compromise who you are, your happiness, and your peace of mind just to be with someone else. It's not worth it. In fact, it's a complete waste of time. Because the time you spend trying to work things out—

You Really Should Already Be Out!

A Strong Woman

A strong woman always knows who she is, and what she wants. She doesn't need anyone to confirm anything for her.

She's confident, courageous and in full control of her own destiny. She remains in the driver's seat at all times. She always has the ability to recognize her strength even when she's weak.

She can recognize what makes her happy even when she's sad. And she can recognize when she's had enough—even when she's willing to continue to take more.

The time has come to get out of your own way—stop the crying, and start the healing.

It has never been him! It has always been you!

Be strong and take full control of the *POWER* in your life, and never relinquish your *Heart or Mind* to anyone!

Handling your business

A strong sense of self is not called being selfish—
it's called handling your business.

A woman and her money

A woman that makes her own money makes her own rules!
Never depend on someone else for your total financial support—because a
woman that has stock, and invests in herself will always receive the best
dividends her money can buy!

Rainbows

Most times the rainbows in our lives can't fully form, and show all the bright colors we have within—this is because we hold onto clouded memories that should have been cleared away a long time ago.

Everyone has a rainbow inside of them; if we allow the rays from the sun to come in and shine through.

Past and Future

The time has come to release all things and people in your life that have caused
you pain or unhappiness.

Make a conscious decision today that you've had enough.

Never allow anyone to take you mentally you don't want to end up physically
or emotionally.

Anger only affects the person that's harboring it.

And the longer you allow it to feaster inside of you the enemy remains in
control and continues to win.

If someone or something isn't adding to the quality of your life then that means
they're taking away from it.

Focus on converting your mountains into streams of water.

Allow all your pain to flow out of your mind and body downstream like the
pebbles of the ocean.

You can't appreciate where you're going until you first recognize where
you've been. The past is a building block for your future.

Therefore, use it as a guide—but never allow it to be your *Excuse!*

Loving Yourself

Loving yourself unconditionally is the best love of all, and there's no one qualified to do a better job for **YOU** than **YOU**!

Inside verses Outside

The way you feel on the inside is what shows on the outside, and confidence goes a long way. Also remember, the way you felt yesterday isn't the same way you must feel today.

Get the most out of each day God has blessed you with, and use it as an opportunity to start fresh and anew.

The Ride

When the ride gets too tough for you to handle that's when you let go and let

God carry you the rest of the way.

God never promised us our lives would be easy.

We can only hope it would be fair!

Dreams

You get out of life exactly what you put into it. If you put a little in then you'll get a little out.

Never stop dreaming, because your dreams are the footprints that will lead you directly towards your future.

Balance

Balance is an important ingredient for a successful and happy life. So
remember if you work hard; you have to play even harder!
Always take time out for yourself, because no one will love, and take care of
you better than you will!

Mistakes

In order to move forward in your life you must be able to face and accept the
mistakes you've made along the way.

But what's most important is not just realizing the mistakes you've made—but
not making the same mistakes over and over again.

Because making the same decisions time after time is no longer considered a
MISTAKE—it's considered your *CHOICE!*

Change

In order for change to be permanent a change must first happen on the inside of you—anything else is strictly on the surface and it won't last.

Let Him Go

When you can no longer recognize the man you once loved and the only things
you have to hold onto are the memories of how things used to be—
Love yourself more, and *Let Him Go*!
It may not be easy—but it's just that simple!

Best Friends

"B" *stands for the bond we share.*

"E" *stands for all the emotions you've supported me through; Rather I wanted to laugh, cry, scream or shout; you've always been there for me and had my back.*

"S" *stands for the strength you've given me when I was weak.*

"T" *stands for the test of time our friendship has endured.*

"F" *stands for the freedom I have when we share our deepest secrets.*

"R" *stands for the relief I feel after we talk.*

"I" *stands for imagine—because I can't imagine having anyone else for a best friend other than you.*

"E" *stands for the eternity of our friendship.*

"N" *stands for nothing—because there's nothing that will ever come between us.*

"D" *stands for the dedication you have to me.*

"S" stands for the solid foundation that our friendship is built on.

Some people give us memories for a short time. Others give us memories for a lifetime. I'm so grateful the memories we share will last until the end of time.

What's for You

What's for you is only for you, and not anyone else!!! But you have to go and get it—because even the milk man doesn't deliver to your door anymore!

Your Cup

When you know your cup is low, and your plate is full. Evaluate the difference between what's good *to* you, and what's good *for* you. However, sometimes it's best to change your menu all together.

Strangers

Sometimes the people that are closest to you are truly the real strangers in your life.

At times their faces are like clouds in the sky that have no real form or meaning; even though you can see them clearly, and you know them well.

Make a pledge today to eliminate all the negative people out of your life.

Surround yourself with positive and supportive people that encourage you, bring out the very best in you and make you happy.

Life is to short to settle, and accept anything less than that!

Test of Life

It's always easier to prepare for the test than it is to take and pass the test. In life all of us will have to prepare for something, and some things will affect us more profoundly and be more important to us than others.

However, the only way to ensure success is to prepare, study, and learn as we go along the way.

Make sure when it's your time to be tested that you're well prepared, and you can stay the course.

It's always easier to take what's given to you. However, it's more satisfying, and fulfilling when you earn it and beat the odds.

Always remember the only person that can stop *YOU* is *YOU!*

Anything or anyone else is truly irrelevant, and standing in your way!

25 Cents

When I was a child twenty-five cents went a long way. Twenty-five cents would buy me twenty-five cookies at the corner store. It would also buy me candy,

ice-cream or even a soda.

Now that life has gotten complicated and it's changed so much; so has the value we put on material things.

Most of us tend to get wrapped up in our wants that we forget all about our needs. We tend to lose focus on the things that really matter and mean the most to us in life.

We begin to equate the quality of our lives with the quantity of things we acquire in life.

If we don't proceed with caution we will spend our entire lives preparing a cake, but never adding the main ingredient.

Stay true to who you are, and what you stand for. Never let the desires of the world take control over the desires of your heart.

Never forgetting the things in life that control you mentally will also control you physically and emotionally.

Your Eyes

Your eyes hold the key that unlocks the mysteries of your soul. Whenever someone looks into your eyes they can read a lot about your story. If there's hurt being harbored; it can be seen there. If you're happy; it can be seen there. If you're struggling with something; it can be seen there.

When there's pain; it too can be seen there.

So if you're curious, and want to know the truth about someone's story or the journey's they've taken in life take one moment and look into their eyes. As their eyes hold the key that unlocks the mysteries of their heart and soul.

Missing You

Every time I hear the birds chirp—I miss your voice. Every time I go to sleep—I miss your presence. Every time I smell cologne—I miss your scent.

Every time I hear the phone ring—I miss our talks.

There was so much I missed about you—I could go on forever and a day if I wanted to.

However, during all those somber nights, and what seemed like endless days while I was missing you—I almost forgot about losing *ME*.

The Big C

I remember that day like it was yesterday—when the doctor said "You have Cancer". My first thoughts were I'm going to die. It was like my heart stopped, and the world that I once knew no longer existed, at least not to me.

Then my mind began to play tricks on me, and without a moment's notice I began to question God and ask him why me? I never expected this dreadful thing to happen especially to me.

Nevertheless, this is part of my life forever. It's my reality. I've always known that everything that happens to us in life isn't fair, and something's we can't even explain.

So, after I cried and prayed, and prayed and cried I finally heard God speak to me. God said, "Cancer may have started this battle—but you'll have the victory." It was then I decided since I know how to pray—I need to stop worrying!

And whether my life consist of five years or just one more day I'm going to live my life to its fullest, and be as happy as I can possibly be—despite what's going on inside of me.

I had to condition my mind to stop focusing on things in my life that were out of my control and I could not change.

I begin to realize that every obstacle in our lives isn't meant to be moved.

Some obstacles are symbolic to strong chains. They have a tight hold on us, and we can't seem to muster up the strength to break away from them.

We have to dig way deep down, hold on tight and ask God to deliver us strength to break free from them. These are the obstacles we have to pray for the strength to go around.

It was then I decided to decrease, and let God increase by strengthening my Mind, Heart, Body and Soul. And since this journey was going to be too long for me to travel all alone—I decided to let go, and let GOD carry me the rest of the way.

I thought to myself. Wow, now I really know what it means to pray.

I decided to take the focus away from the big "C", and put it all back on me!

During the weakest times of our lives God has our back, and he's only one prayer away. But in order to receive, we first must have *Faith, Trust* and *Believe*.

Remember –

God doesn't want us to be Fearful. He wants us to be Strengthen, Empowered and Encouraged

Waste of Time

It's a complete waste of time trying to change another person, put that time into yourself—because the time you spend trying to figure things out— God's already worked them out!

Success

Success is desired by many—but only obtained by few. In this game called life they're players and they're winners. It's up to you to decide what side of the playing field you want to be on.

Unfortunately, the tricks of this game aren't taught; they're learned. And it's not considered a true opportunity unless you take full advantage of all your options.

Therefore, take mental notes along the way, and use them throughout your life to help you understand what rules you want to play by, and what works best for you.

Always understanding that behind every disappointment is a new opportunity for success.

And our shortcomings are not considered failures. They serve as stepping-stones and reminders of what we could do better the next time around.

Never let anyone place mental or physical boundaries on your abilities—
because in order to get to the stars; you must first reach for the sky!

Butterfly

When I saw the butterfly slightly resting on the tree—it reminded me of how simple life could truly be.

I know it may sound strange to you, and to me to grasp a concept so plain and free.

But you will understand once you finally see the innocence of a butterfly resting slightly on the tree.

Imperfection

I never wanted to be a perfect person. That would be a job to big for me—because life is full of to many struggles, heartbreaks and uncertainty.

So instead of striving for perfection I strive to be the best I can possibly be—because to me this is truly the key to being happy, at peace and living in tranquility.

Little Sister

I never realized how special you were to me. When you were a little girl and always wanted to follow me. Oh how I wish we could go back in time just to spend a little more time talking, playing games, and having fun like sisters really ought to be.

Unfortunately, like everything else in our lives that move so fast—so has the innocence from those good old days that have passed, and all we have left to cherish are our precious memories.

Now we're all grown up with kids of our own I can finally see how special those moments really were to me—all those times you reached out and asked could you please follow me.

Love

There's something special about being in love you see.

To have that special someone to love you, kiss you, or simply hold you tight when you're in need.

I can't imagine how empty my life would be if you were not here to comfort me.

Even though these words often go unspoken—please understand you will always be my *Peace*, my *Rock*, and my right *Hand*.

And I will always *Love, Trust,* and be here for you as long as I can breathe.

Xanadu

When the trip you're on is no longer worth the journey—it's time to change
your destination, and find your Xanadu.
No one can change your direction in life without you being in the driver's seat
and ultimately controlling the path, and direction you're traveling.
Spend more time getting to know who *YOU* really are.
Discover what works best for you. This is something only you can do.
Because everyone needs a special place to call their own
secret Xanadu.

Other Books by Author:

Flip the Script: Why does it always have to be about HIM?

Sentiments to Soothe Your Soul

Cookbook and Novel coming soon

Check website for updates and Play information.

www.hallpublishinggroup.com